Nourishing the Grieving Heart

Nourishing the Grieving Heart

Reflections and Paths for Healing

Jane L. Thompson, MSW
with Holly Cashin

Empath Press, LLC
Minneapolis

Empath Press, LLC
empathpress.com

Design by Dorie McClelland, springbookdesign.com
Printed in Canada by Friesens.

ISBN: 978-0-9889531-0-9

Permissions:
Page 40, The Fall of Freddie the Leaf, Buscaglia L. Reprinted with permission from SLACK Incorporated: Thorofare, NJ: SLACK Incorporated; 1982
Page 7, from HEALING INTO LIFE AND DEATH by Stephen Levine, copyright ©1987 by Stephen Levine. Used by permission of Doubleday, a division of Random House, Inc.

Photo Credits:
Holly Cashin, page 44
Jan Rabbers, pages 4, 8, 12, 19, 27, 28, 34, 36, 38, 42
Lunderby Photography, page v
Patricia G. Swantek, cover and page 40
Jane Thompson, page 11
Devin Aadland, page 49

Dedication

This book is dedicated to the memory of our firstborn son, Timmy, whose vibrant life unexpectedly ended due to a boating accident.

Our love and longing for him never ceases. Yet our souls are refreshed when we remember his cheery and gregarious nature. He embraced life fully and was adored by his two brothers. His involvement in high school and college was tireless. Indeed, his life was both short and lived well. His legacy of love remains always. — *Holly Cashin*

Introduction

After many years of meeting with others as a psychotherapist, as well as navigating through several personal losses, I am convinced that there are two requirements for us to find a healing path through grief:

   We need to give expression to the deep feelings that can fill every corner of our being and know that it is sacred to allow others to bear witness to our sorrow.

   In the following pages we have collected reflections of myriad circumstances of loss and grief. In each, we offer suggested pathways for healing through various forms of expression.

   The paths may be taken as described or used as inspiration to form new passages that resonate more personally.

— Jane Thompson

When the death of my son threw me into the unfamiliar role of a grieving mother, I discovered there were certain powerful concepts and images that soothed my aching soul.

   Words, thoughts and rituals often carried me through each week.

   By sharing this collection of grief reflections and expressions, it is my desire that others might similarly ease their pathways toward healing.

— Holly Cashin

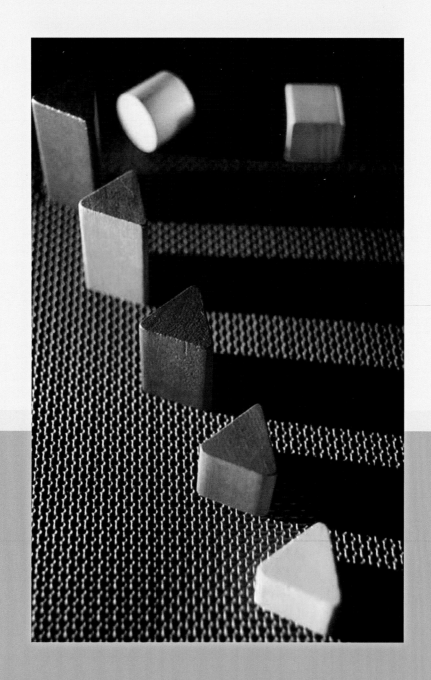

The Geometry of Loss

Losses come to us in many shapes and colors, and sometimes we are taken into grief by shapes that everyone can identify with, such as death or the end of a precious relationship. These are, perhaps, the recognizable searing red circle or black shape of a teardrop or a heart.

Many shapes and colors of loss are not so easily discerned and the grief that accompanies them can look very unfamiliar or remain almost invisible. The loss of a job, the loss of health, the loss of a dream, or the loss of dignity, to name a few. Sometimes we don't see the broken places in the lives of those around us.

When we do recognize another's loss, it may resonate with some part of our own life experience and there can be a sudden wish to pull back from looking further. Invisible grief and unnamed losses are inescapable and yet we aren't accustomed to attending to the wounds they cause. These are losses for which there are no pre-printed sympathy cards.

Grief visits all of us . . . often. We live with it, and through it, and are asked to bear witness to it in others.

Everyone's loss is, for them, the hardest.

A Path to Consider

You might wonder or ask: What does my friend grieve? Does he or she have a loss that's gone unrecognized by me? What are the unique shapes and colors of loss in our human community?

Lost Dreams

As we move through our sorrow, we're flooded with memories of our loved one and the times we shared. Images return accompanied by sweet smiles and salty tears. Soon we also come to know that we are also grieving lost dreams. We're faced with releasing bundles of hopes, milestone occasions, planned events, and shared times that will no longer be realized in the way we had looked forward to.

A Path to Consider

Name the dreams, the hopes, the plans. For each one send it off with a blown bubble or a puff on a feathery dandelion. Send it off with a blessing.
   Re-imagine what dreams are still possible without the physical presence of our loved one.

Reflection

Grief Stings

"Grief is the rope burns left when something we have held most dearly has been pulled out of our reach, beyond our grasp."

— Stephen Levine

A Path to Consider

Visualize your pain as rope burns. Take a few minutes to let warm water run through your palms or gently massage a soothing lotion onto your hands. Tend to the injury and trust that the sting will lessen with time.

Now I Lay Me Down to Sleep

". . . and my heart seems to be breaking. I miss you and feel as if I will split in half from the sheer longing. I need to feel you with me now."

A Path to Consider

Think about something you could place inside your pillowcase this night to help you feel the closeness of the one you are missing . . . a scarf, a mitten, a t-shirt, some memento?

We Will Not Fall

At those times when we feel vulnerable and utterly without strength, we need reminders that in grief we are upheld by our own faith in concert with the caring of others. From day to day, our fragile hearts rest on that foundation. We can trust the delicate balance and know that we will not fall.

A Path to Consider

Gather smooth pebbles. Make a cairn. Be reminded that you are upheld even when all feels uncertain; you will not fall.

Love Letters

Even though we may try our best to speak from our hearts and say the important things to those we love, we never get it "all said." Time after time, the thought comes back, "I wish I could say 'I love you' one more time" or "Thank you" or "Did you know . . . ?" or "I'm sorry" or ". . ."

A Path to Consider

It is never too late to write our love letters. We don't need fancy journals, and our words are not for others to read. Whenever you feel inclined, take any paper and give voice to your heart's message. Write your love letter and then shred it if you wish. It's not necessarily a document to be saved, but rather a message from your heart to the soul of another.

How Do I Know I'm Healing?

Grief is so painful and we long to know how we can tell that we're healing . . . and when it will happen.

Soon after a loss, the awareness of that which is missing is directly in the middle of our field of vision. It is the lens through which we view everything. It colors everything and we don't know how to change its position. As time passes, there is a little movement to the side, and still later, that image of grief may show up mostly in our peripheral vision. We turn to look at it, or it taps us on the shoulder.

A Path to Consider

Now and then, close your eyes and try to imagine where your grief is located at this moment. Is it to the side or right in front of you? Notice when there are more times that it seems to be slightly off to the side, and then be assured you are healing.

Being Strong

After a loss, how many times do we tell ourselves that we must be strong? Does that mean we must choke back the tears, tell others that we're okay and return back to work as soon as possible? We want to do our very best to hang on and also help those who share our loss to move forward. We want the feeling of *normal* back, even though everything has changed. We want others to support us yet not burden them and we need, somehow, to convince ourselves we will survive this.

A Path to Consider

It takes enormous courage to grieve. Strength is not the absence of tears or anger, of sobs and clenched fists. Being strong requires us to be real, to allow our tears and laments to pour forth and to recognize that being authentic is the greatest tribute. This will anchor us and those who share our sorrow.

Reflection

Unspoken Conversations

It is very rare after we lose someone dear that we don't, from time to time, think to ourselves, "Oh, I must remember to tell her about this" or "When I get home I want to be sure to ask him about . . ."

These are the times when we might find ourselves picking up our phone to call and then feel stunned by the harsh awareness there will be no more calls. Each of these moments of grief arrive with needle-point sharpness.

A Path to Consider

Pause. Call someone who cares for you and is supportive. Tell them your news, or simply share the fact that you are longing to be in touch with the one you have lost. Allow yourself to express your grief and receive the warmth of another person bearing witness to your sorrow at these ordinary moments.

19

The Boulder

"When is it going to get better?" she said. To that, "What would better be like?" I replied.
"Three years have gone by since he passed and I still feel so sad."
"Did you think it would be different by now?"
"Well, yes. Others told me how time heals and it would become easier."

I have come to believe that grief is rather like finding ourselves weighted down by a
100-pound boulder. We often live with the hope that in time it will become lighter.
In fact, it remains the same size. However, we do learn to carry it with greater ease and
balance. We develop new muscles. Sometimes we carry it in a backpack. Other times we
allow someone else to carry it with us.

A Path to Consider

Perhaps a small pebble in your pocket or purse may become a reminder of this boulder
and also a reminder that you can find ways to carry it and still live fully.

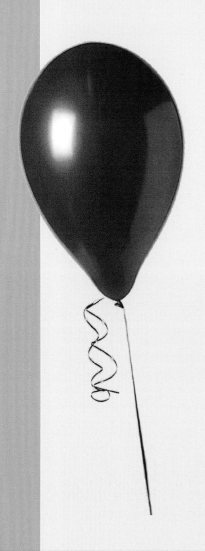

Reflection

The Red Balloon

I met Jamie's parents a month after he had died at the tender age of three years old. Jamie, they told me, loved balloons, especially red ones. The bigger, the better!

Just prior to Jamie's passing, an appointment had been scheduled for a family portrait. They intended to cancel it, confessing they could not even imagine doing a family photo again. We talked a long time and, after much reflection, they did indeed follow through. In my holiday card that year was a picture: Mom, Dad, two sisters and a red balloon. For the past 23 years each family photo has a red balloon somewhere!

A Path to Consider

Reminders—balloons, toys, a certain color, a class ring, a song, a favorite slipper, a coffee mug . . . is this a way you can continue to make visible the spirit of your loved one?

Delete?

I found myself going through the list of contacts on my cell phone. A routine sort of act when there she was! Lesley, followed by her cell phone number, work phone number, and address. My beloved friend, Lesley died almost two years ago. A wash of sadness poured over me and then the question, "Do I delete her?" I can't phone her and yet the thought of eliminating her contact information seemed undoable, so wrong to me.

My peace returned when I went to the awareness that of course I would remove nothing for, in fact, I will hold this as a clear reminder of her loving presence in my life, the effects of which are not muted by her death.

I hope, as time goes on, I feel less of a sting and open to a wash of gratitude when next I stumble upon Lesley in my contacts.

A Path to Consider

Healing is not at all about forgetting. Rather, it serves us sometimes to embrace and carry things that will jar our memories or afford us the opportunity to affirm that the goodness of another stays with us past the date of any ending.

Reflection

Hold On

"Hang in there," people tell me. "Just hang in there." As I'm hanging in there, what is it that I'm to hold to? My dear one is gone. My dreams are shattered, and there is no compass for this journey. What can I possibly hang on to?

A Path to Consider

Gather up each and every memory and object that reminds you or helps you feel a sense of connection. Hang on to the certainty that when we cherish another, something of them remains with us even in their absence. Hold his golf clubs, hang on to her keychain, put his cap on and hold close that pillow.

Finally, hold near to you the people who love you, those who will steadfastly bear witness and walk this path of grief with you.

The Tears May Never Stop

"I'm afraid that if I let myself cry, the tears will never stop."

These are the words frequently shared when someone is feeling unbearable sorrow. These are the words said when one feels a lump in the throat that almost chokes even though months, even years, have passed.

A Path to Consider

When we laugh, we never worry that the laughter will never end. Is it not also true that each and every expression is naturally limited? We will not laugh or cry, shout or gasp without end. In that knowledge, let your tears flow . . . you will not crumble. Rather in the release, you'll find yourself opening to nuggets of hope.

Grief Is Not About Letting Go

Our memories become connections to the one we are missing. A young man once said to me that he would "never again eat macaroni and cheese and not think of his mom because she made the best." To this day, it is what he chooses for his birthday dinner and he's teaching his son how to follow the recipe!

So often we hear people refer to the goal of grief as "letting go." On the contrary, grief asks us to integrate loss and find ways to carry with us the memories and experiences of the person we grieve.

A Path to Consider

List some memories, ideas, places, recipes, activities, items and beliefs that you will not be letting go of . . . and then share them with someone else.

The Mailbox

A client told me about a recent trip to London. She's a jogger and wherever she travels she tends to go for a morning run followed by coffee, preferably at an outdoor table. While enjoying an espresso on her recent trip, she saw a metal display holding picture postcards. She looked through a number of them and was drawn to a particular view of Hyde Park.

She returned to her table having purchased the card and began writing to her mother about this lovely time in London. Her mom had died 13 years ago.

Continuing with her story, she told me it's her practice, when away and experiencing the beauty of a new place, to select a card, buy a stamp, address it to "MOM," then place it in the nearest mailbox.

In this expression, she honors their relationship and feels better not trying to squelch the wish to send a card to the person who remains very much alive in her heart.

A Path to Consider

Remember, there are no rules about how we live with loss, how we grieve, and what opens us to the healing that may come from an expressive act. Go ahead . . . no one's looking!

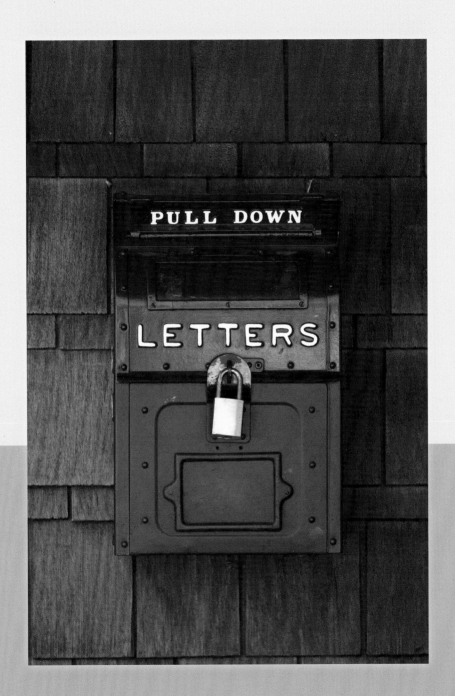

Reflection

The Holidays Are Coming

"My heart is filled with longing for your presence. I want to find some way for you to be part of our holiday traditions now that you are gone.

"How will we feast at a table when your place is empty? Can we light candles without the teardrops extinguishing them? Can we say the usual blessings and prayers without choking on each word? What about the Christmas tree or the Menorah?"

A Path to Consider

Embrace each tradition authentically. Let the tears flow if they do, and the smiles as well. Remember times passed, name out loud the one you are missing. Bless them with a spirit of gratitude and honoring.

Brokenness to Beauty

As we come upon our own time of grief, we soon recognize our brokenness. Our hearts feel shattered and we no longer find it easy to believe that we will ever again know beauty and wholeness.

A Path to Consider

Find a sculpture of clay, a porcelain heart or a brightly colored glass vase. Place one of these in a heavy-duty sealed plastic bag and break it! Hold onto those pieces for a while and, when the time is right, make of them a mosaic or place them at the bottom of a clear vase to shine beneath the fresh flowers it holds. Consider it a sign of transformation and hope.

Grief's Lost and Found

This grief journey always begins with the awareness of loss—gut-wrenching, heartbreaking loss. Those experiences of loss may continue and, yet, we find moments of grace, new insights, loving gestures from friends and even occasional laughter. We lose much and we find much.

A Path to Consider

Bear witness to the losses you experience and also to the experiences of finding or reclaiming. Gather a box and make it your personal "lost and found." Write about the difficult losses as well as the gentle finds and place them here together for safekeeping.

The Fall of Freddie the Leaf

"It's what happens in Fall," Daniel told them. "It's the time for leaves to change their home. Some people call it to die."

"Will we all die?" Freddie asked.

"Yes," Daniel answered. "Everything dies. No matter how big or small, how weak or strong. We first do our job. We experience the sun and the moon, the wind and the rain. We learn to dance and to laugh. Then we die."

"Where will we go when we die?"
"No one knows for sure. That's the great mystery!"
"Will we return in the Spring?"
"We may not but Life will."
— Leo Buscaglia

A Path to Consider

Walk a wooded path in autumn, fill a bowl with fallen leaves, hold one to the light and remember, "life will return."

Reflection

Images of Your Beloved

How many times, as we move through our lives with someone, do we notice their reflection can be seen with our own reflection in the mirror? There are also those times when we walk down a sidewalk and see shadows of both of us just ahead of our feet. Now, in this loss, we pass a store window and see only the solitary self mirrored back to us.

   Where is that other person now?

A Path to Consider

Find a mirror and place a photo of the person you are missing on half of it. Look into it and see again the reflection of your relationship, your love and your beloved.
   Remember, also, that you are, on your own, a whole and complete person.

Reflection

We Can't Lose What We've Loved

"What we have enjoyed we can never lose. All that we love becomes a part of us."

— Helen Keller

There is a need to affirm and hold dear the love we have shared with the person we've lost.

A Path to Consider

Pause and call forth a sweet memory today. What images do you remember? Close your eyes and picture that which you hold dear and trust it can never be taken from you. Recall the blessing and feel the gratitude.

Our Memories Become Bridges

In our loneliness we want to feel the connection again and memories become bridges for those who grieve. Each time we recall a heartwarming story, look at a photograph, reminisce about our loved one or hear a particular song, memories are brought forward and we are again linked in a loving way to the one we miss.

A Path to Consider

Tell your stories over and over. Write them. Listen to the music that brings you close to them, and see once more the many things you saw with one another . . . and remember.

Acknowledgments

This book has been writing itself for years. I think back to the rich experience of leading a weekly therapy group for over fifteen years with women facing recurrent or advanced-stage cancer. Their dear voices still speak to me. I hope in some small way this book continues to honor the many folks who have allowed me to be with them as they came to their deaths . . . and to those who continue to love them.

My gratitude for the creative, heartfelt, and dedicated support offered always to me by Jan. She has been a compassionate witness to my own grief and invited me to enter the sacred space of her own.

Finally, Holly has been the person who has deeply blessed this work with her energy, her heart, her honesty, and her courage. She has kept company with grief and continues to embrace life in its fullest with reverence and hope. — *Jane*

My deep thanks to Tim whose enthusiasm, zest, and generosity have affirmed this project. My eternal gratitude to him for holding my hand as we journey through our grief together.

Enormous gratitude to my understanding and steadfast friend, Pat. Her honest feedback and insights have been a gift.

And to Jane, an infinite source of wisdom and inspiration. She is truly a dear friend with rare qualities of eloquence, compassion, strength, and gentleness. — *Holly*

The Authors

Jane Thompson, MSW

began practicing psychotherapy after she completed her graduate studies at Saint Louis University in 1975. Her career has chiefly focused upon counseling the bereaved, while guiding individuals and families as they meet the challenges of chronic and life-threatening illnesses. She has accompanied clients as they moved through various life transitions and the losses they incur.

Throughout Jane's career, she has regarded her clients as teachers and collaborators in her own journey. She sincerely values the privilege of being allowed to be a compassionate presence in the journeys of others.

Besides her rich professional life in Minneapolis, she enjoys reading, Pilates, drawing, and the company of those dear to her.

Her website is www.empathpress.com, where she invites readers to participate in an ongoing dialogue.

Holly Cashin

is a graduate of the University of Minnesota and has worked professionally as a physical therapist for 25 years. Her role working with disabled children and adults has been immensely fulfilling and given her much insight into the grief experienced with the loss of physical abilities.

She has raised three active and healthy boys that kept her on her toes for many years.

Holly is now retired from her work as a physical therapist and spends her leisure time traveling with her family, reading, gardening, and socializing.